W9-AUV-414

Information/artwork is outdated

EDUCATION LIBRARY
UNIVERSITY OF KENTUCKY

The
EXTINCT

Alphabet Book

by Jerry Pallotta   illustrated by Ralph Masiello

EDUC
JE
PAL

EDUCATION LIBRARY
UNIVERSITY OF KENTUCKY

AG07441

Thank you to John P. Meehan, Charles Magliozzi, Joe Napolitano, John Granese, Lucien Rousseau, Frank Mastrocola, Jr., Lou Borgatti, and Lou Barrett for teaching me all about the business world.

Jerry Pallotta
Peggotty Beach, 1993

I would like to dedicate these illustrations to my daughter, Alexa, and my niece, Morgan. . . . Special thanks to Dr. Duke Dawson at the New England Science Center.

Ralph Masiello
Ickybugville, 1993

Copyright © 1993
by Jerry Pallotta.
Illustrations Copyright © 1993
by Ralph Masiello.
All rights reserved,
including the right of reproduction
in whole or in part in any form.

Published by
Charlesbridge Publishing
85 Main Street
Watertown, MA 02172
(617) 926-0329

Printed in the United States of America
(sc) 10 9 8 7 6 5 4 3 2 1
(hc) 10 9 8 7 6 5 4 3 2 1
(lb) 10 9 8 7 6 5 4 3 2 1

Thank you to the Burgess Shale creatures for appearing in this book.

All illustrations in this book were painted with brushes using oil paints on primed and stretched canvas.

Printed on Recycled Paper.

Books by Jerry Pallotta:
The Icky Bug Alphabet Book
The Icky Bug Counting Book
The Bird Alphabet Book
The Ocean Alphabet Book
The Flower Alphabet Book
The Yucky Reptile Alphabet Book
The Frog Alphabet Book
The Furry Alphabet Book
The Dinosaur Alphabet Book
The Underwater Alphabet Book
The Victory Garden Alphabet Book
Going Lobstering
Cuenta los insectos (The Icky Bug Counting Book)

Library of Congress Cataloging-in-Publication Data
Pallotta, Jerry.
   The extinct alphabet book / by Jerry Pallotta: illustrated by Ralph Masiello.
      p.   cm.
   Summary: Each letter of the alphabet features information about a creature that no longer exists.
   ISBN 0-88106-686-9 (library reinforced)
   ISBN 0-88106-471-8 (hardcover)
   ISBN 0-88106-470-X (softcover)
   1. Extinct animals—Juvenile literature. 2. English language—Alphabet—Juvenile literature. [1. Rare animals. 2. Alphabet.] I. Masiello, Ralph, ill. II. Title.
QL88.P34 1993
591.52'9 — dc20
                                        93-1512
                                           CIP
                                            AC

A is for Alphabet Book.
A is also for Akioloa. The cute Akioloa
birds used to live in Hawaii. They
became extinct after they caught a
bird disease.

The word extinct means "no longer
in existence" or "died out."
The creatures in this book
no longer live on Earth.

A a

B b

B is for Blue Buck. Blue Bucks were not really blue. As they grew older, the combination of their gray and white hair made them appear blue. Blue Bucks became extinct when people killed them for dog food.

C is for Coelecanth. The name of this fish is pronounced SEE-la-kanth. Everyone, especially the paleontologists, thought that Coelecanths had disappeared from the face of the Earth seventy million years ago. But in 1938 a Coelecanth was caught alive. What a surprise! This fish was never extinct and should not be in this book.

Cc

Cc

C is also for Coelurosauravus. This name is so hard to pronounce we will just call him "Chuckie." "Chuckie" was a gliding reptile. Is your new name OK, "Chuckie?"

D d

D is for Dimetrodon. Absolutely, positively no dinosaurs are to be seen or mentioned in this book. The Dimetrodon was not a dinosaur. It was a pelycosaur. All dinosaurs had legs that were directly under their bodies.

E e

E is for Embolotherium. If it had survived, the Embolotherium would have been a good creature to take a ride on. You could sit right up front on its head and hold on tight.

F is for Four-toed Horse. The tiny Four-toed Horse had four toes on each front leg and three toes on each back leg. A more accurate name might have been the Fourteen-toed Horse! That was millions of years ago. Today, horses have hooves. Each hoof is really one big toe.

Ff

G g

G is for
Giant White Shark,
or maybe it was a
Giant Black Shark.
This huge, extinct
shark no longer swims
in the ocean. If it did,
everyone in your class
could fit in its mouth. This
illustration is the actual size
of just one of its teeth.

Putting your whole class in the Giant Shark's mouth with all those big, sharp teeth was not such a good idea. Here is a better idea:

H is for Henodus. Your whole class, a few friends, and a couple of cousins could have ridden on the back of this humongous turtle if it were still alive today.

H h

H h

H is also for Hallucigenia. The Hallucigenia was so unusual looking that scientists thought they were hallucinating when they discovered it. Hallucigenia fossils were found embedded in the famous rocks known as the Burgess Shale. Which end do you think was its head?

I i

I is for Irish Elk. The Irish Elk was not an elk and did not live just in Ireland. It used to roam all over Europe. It was the biggest deer that ever lived, and it had the most far-reaching antlers of any animal.

J j

J is for Jamaican Long-tongued Bat. There is only one of these left on Earth. It is dead and is being preserved in a jar of alcohol in Jamaica. We can only imagine how this bat lived when it was alive.

JAMAICAN LONG-TONGUED
BAT

K k

K is for Kaka.
Kaka is the funny name
of a bird that used to live on
Norfolk Island, New Zealand.
If we could go back in time and
talk to this bird it would probably
say, "I wish I had a different
name." Do you think it
would rather be called
Spiderhead?

L l

L is for Las Vegas Frog. Unfortunately, a quick way to make a creature become extinct is to destroy its habitat. It happened. People built the city of Las Vegas and paved over all the fresh water springs where this frog used to live. Sadly, we say good-bye to the Las Vegas Frog.

M is for Moa. This huge bird was almost twice as tall as the tallest basketball players, but it could not fly. Today there is no Moa. Did you know that many people now think some dinosaurs evolved into birds?

M m

N is for Neanderthal Men and Women. It was once thought that Neanderthals were direct ancestors to the human beings of today. Now it is more widely believed that Neanderthals were distant cousins and did not evolve into modern humans. How did they get their name? Their fossils were found in Germany in the valley of the Neander River.

Nn

Would you name this bird an A-A, an E-E, an I-I, an O-O, a U-U or maybe sometimes a Y-Y? The Hawaiian people called this extinct bird an O-O.

O is for O-O.
O-O is a much better name than Uh-Oh or Oh-No!

O o

O is also for Opabinia. Some scientists think every child should learn about the Opabinia because it was a different and unique life form. It had five eyes, a three-piece tail, gills along its sides, and a long trunk with a grasping mouth. What a weirdo!

P is for Platybelodon. Stop and look closely. This is not an elephant! The Platybelodon had two huge teeth on its lower jaw — perfect for scooping vegetation out of the water.

P p

Q q

Q is for Quagga. It is illogical to hunt a species into extinction, however, people hunted and ate all the Quaggas. This beautiful, African mammal had stripes on its neck and head, not all over its body like a zebra. Would you have eaten a quaggaburger?

R is for Round Island Split-jawed Snake. This is one of only two known snakes that ever had a hinged upper jaw. When goats and rabbits were introduced to Round Island, they ate all the grass and trees. The topsoil washed away, and these snakes had no place to live or safely lay their eggs.

R r

S s

S is for Steller's Sea Cow. This huge, toothless mammal weighed up to eight thousand pounds. Sailors on whaling ships considered the red meat of the Steller's Sea Cow to be the best steak in the world. Killing and eating all of them was a serious "mis-steak."

Oops! A spelling mistake.

T is for Tasmanian Wolf.
The last living Tasmanian Wolf
was seen in a zoo. It must have been
sad seeing the last one behind bars and
knowing that there were never going
to be any more. The Tasmanian
Wolf had a pouch just
like the kangaroo.

T t

T t

T is also for Tanystropheus.
It is nice to see a lizard that lived
on the edge and was willing
to stick its neck out.

Here is something to think about:
more than ninety-nine percent of all
living things that ever lived on Earth
are now extinct.

U u

U is for Uh-Oh!
Ralph, the illustrator,
was busy painting when he
tripped and spilled red paint all
over this page. CRASH!
SPLASH! Now this painting is
extinct. The paint wiped out
this illustration forever.

U might have been for
Urogomphus, a giant extinct
dragonfly, or, Undina, an extinct
lobed-finned fish,
or maybe Ula-Ai-Hawane, another
extinct Hawaiian bird.

V is for Vieraella.
The Vieraella is the oldest
known frog. It was alive
85 million years ago. We
are not sure what it looked
like, exactly, but here is
what its fossilized
bones look like.

We know about some
animals only by their
fossils or the bones
they left behind.
Fossilization occurs
when minerals replace
what used to be the
bones of an animal.

V v

W is for White Dodo. Almost everyone knows that Dodo birds are extinct. They used to live peacefully on islands in the Indian Ocean. They had no natural predators until sailors arrived with pigs, monkeys, cats and rats. Eventually, the Dodo birds vanished.

Legend has it that people could walk right up to a Dodo and step on it. Apparently, Dodos were not very smart.

W w

X x

X is for Xerces Blue.
Blue is a type of butterfly.
The Xerces Blue lived on one
small hill in San Francisco.
Unfortunately, as the city expanded,
the trees and bushes where this
butterfly lived were cut down.
The Xerces Blue disappeared forever.

Y is for Yellow-tufted Bee-eater. Why did this extinct bird eat bees? What's wrong with eating other letters of the alphabet, like P's and Q's? Everyone knows peas are good for you!

Y y

Z is for Zygorhiza. Notice that this sea mammal had a neck. Today, dolphins, porpoises, and whales are beautifully streamlined so that they can swim faster.

Zillions of plants and animals lived on Earth and then became extinct over the last four billion years. Imagine how many other species will be extinct in the future. Let's hope human beings never become extinct.

Z z